Nautical Scenes
TO PAINT OR COLOR

DOT BARLOWE

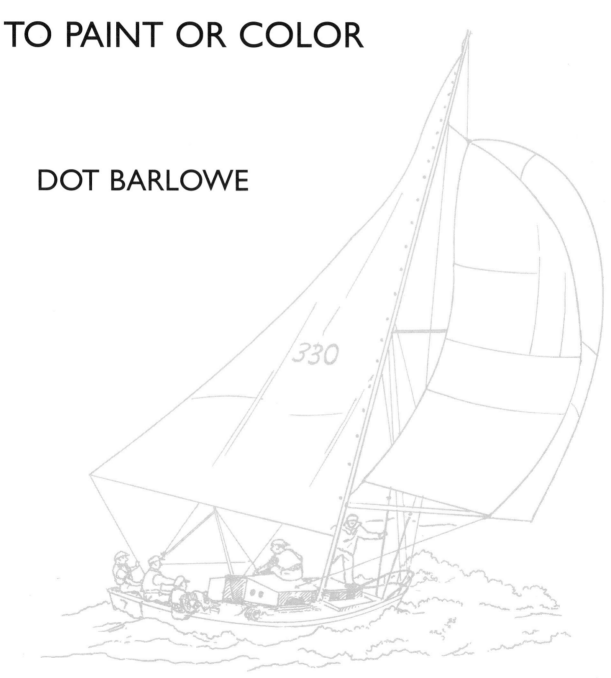

DOVER PUBLICATIONS, INC.
MINEOLA, NEW YORK

Special thanks to my daughter, Amy Barlowe-Bodman,
for her fine photos and for helping me with the
extensive research for this book.

Let the adventurous lure of the sea entice you in this delightful collection of nautical motifs. This vibrant assortment of illustrations includes exciting scenes of powerful ocean waves, a sloop sailing amid dolphins frolicking in the surf, a stately lighthouse on a rocky shore, and a sailboat cast upon some choppy seas. You may also appreciate the calm serenity of the coast, with plates depicting the peace of a New England marina, a panoramic view of a lake and mountains, and a seagull resting on the shore. A variety of different vessels are shown as well, such as a luxury yacht, houseboat, canoe, charter boat, and catamaran. Simply add your own color to bring the natural vitality of these images to stunning life.

Rendered by artist Dot Barlowe, the 23 plates in this book are perforated for easy removal and are printed on one side only, so dark markers and paints will not show through. In addition, the outlines have been printed in a light gray line so that they virtually disappear when painted or colored, resulting in a more polished and professional appearance.

Bibliographical Note
Nautical Scenes to Paint or Color is a new work, first published
by Dover Publications, Inc., in 2007.

International Standard Book Number
ISBN-13: 978-0-486-45693-5
ISBN-10: 0-486-45693-5

Manufactured in the United States by LSC Communications
45693507   2017
www.doverpublications.com

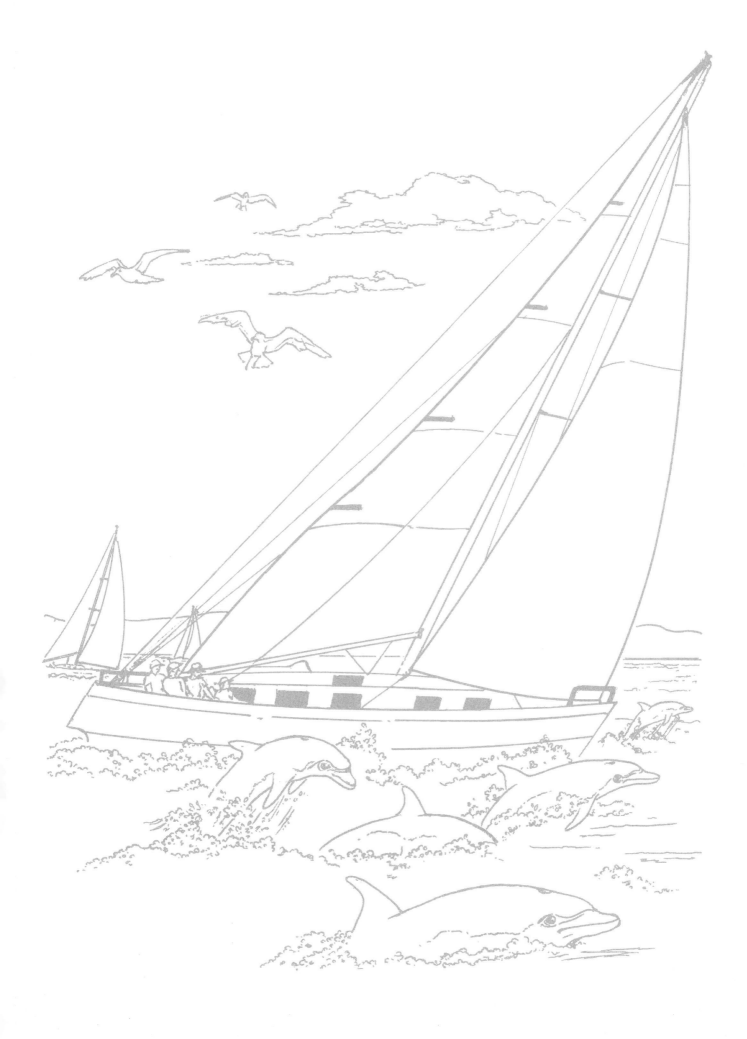

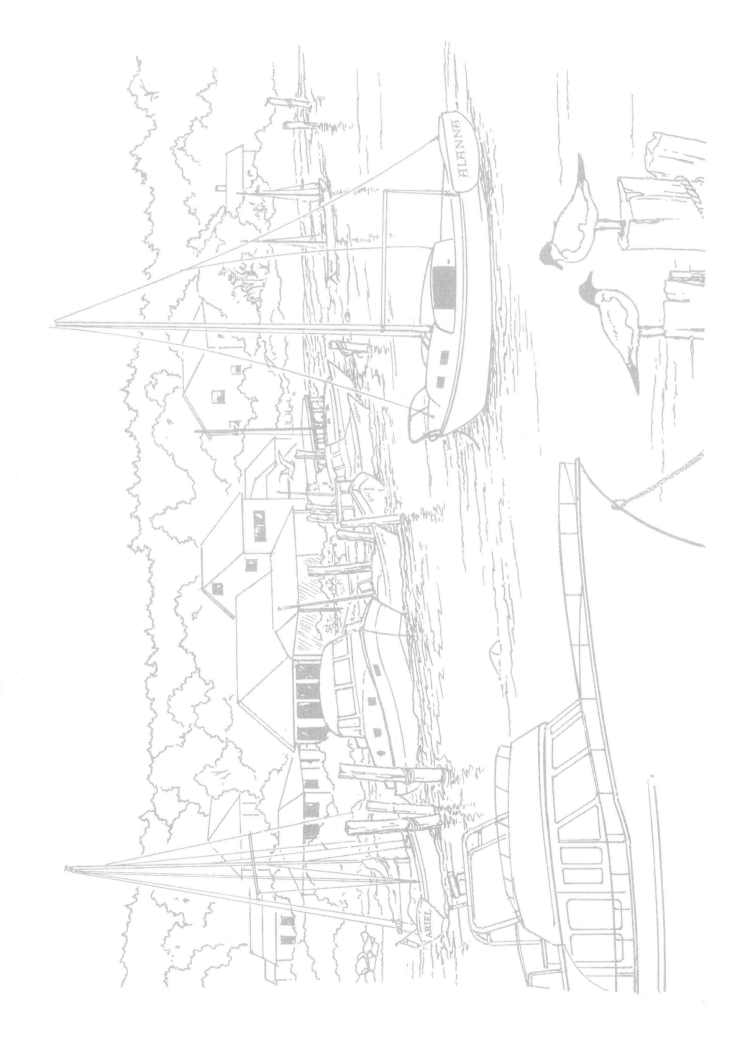

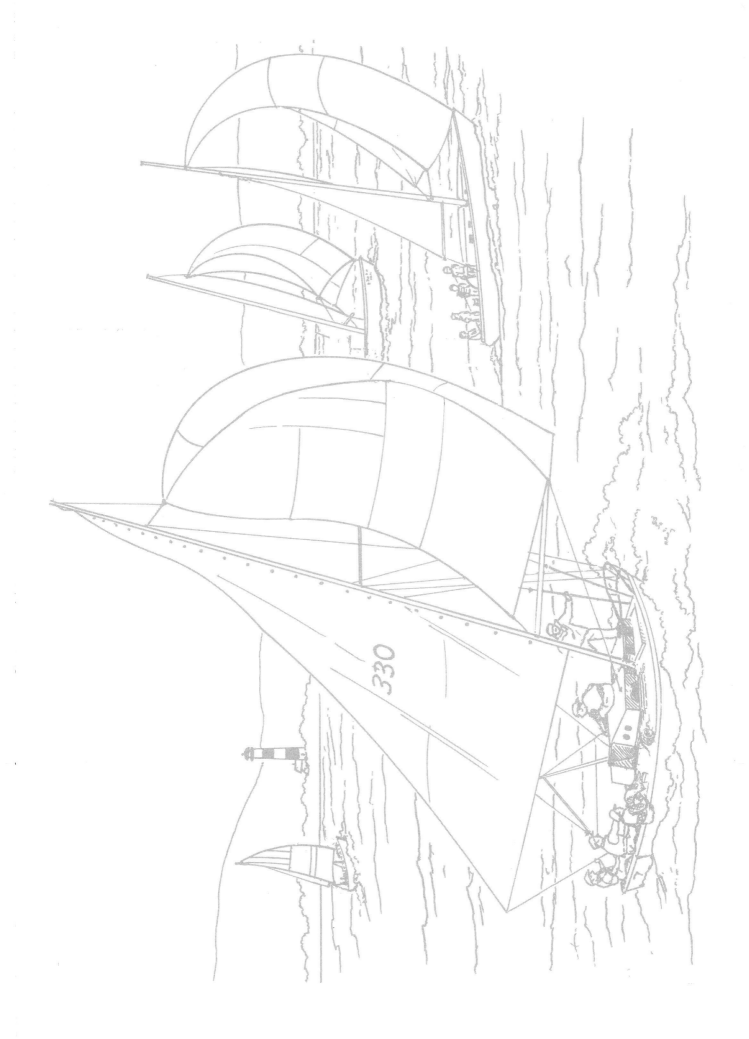

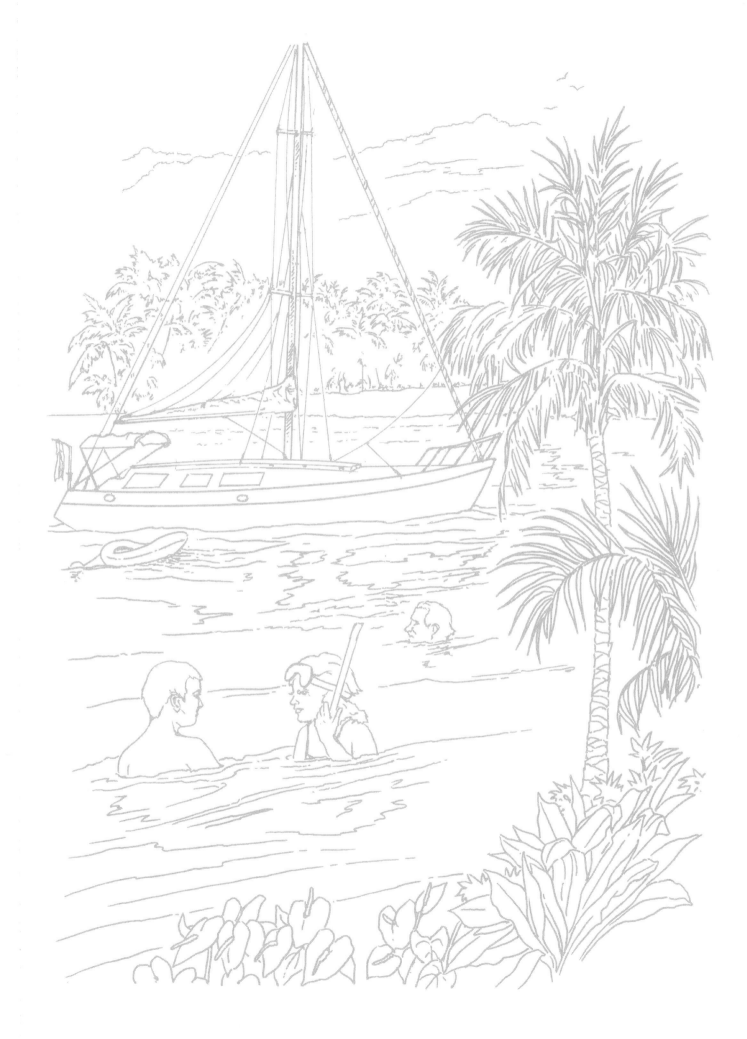

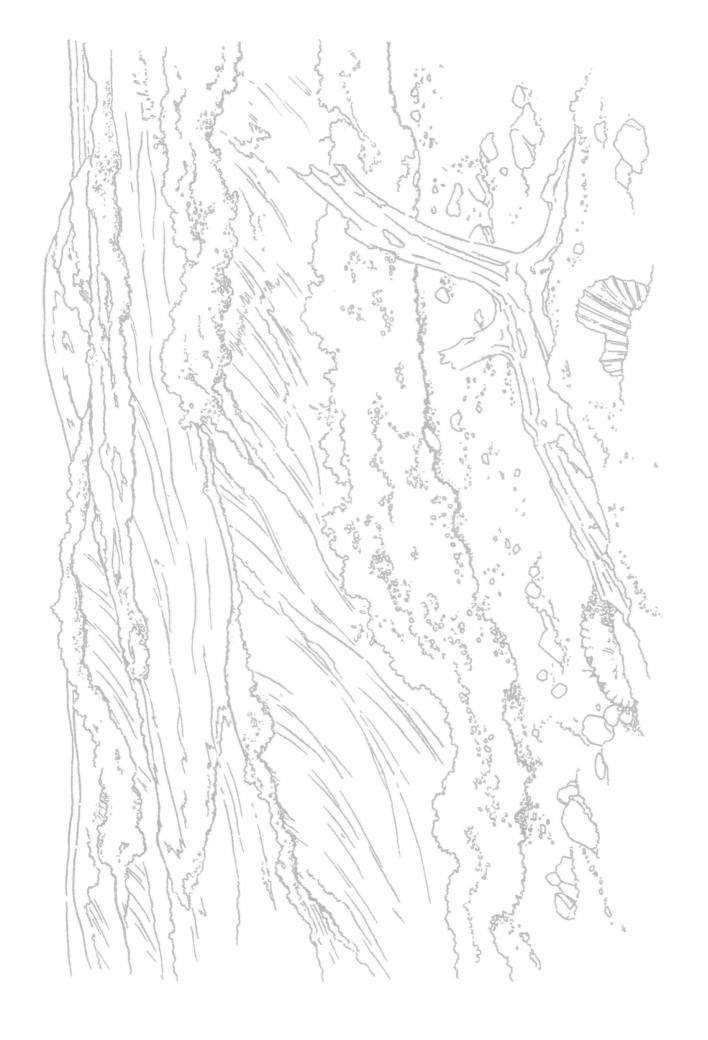

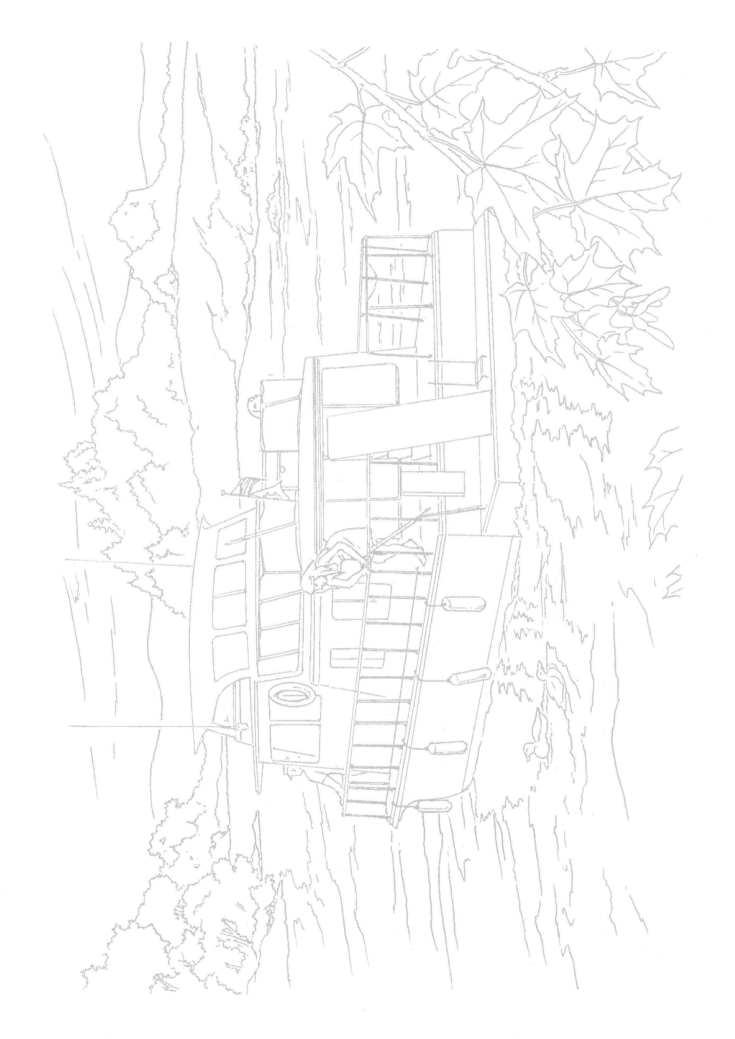

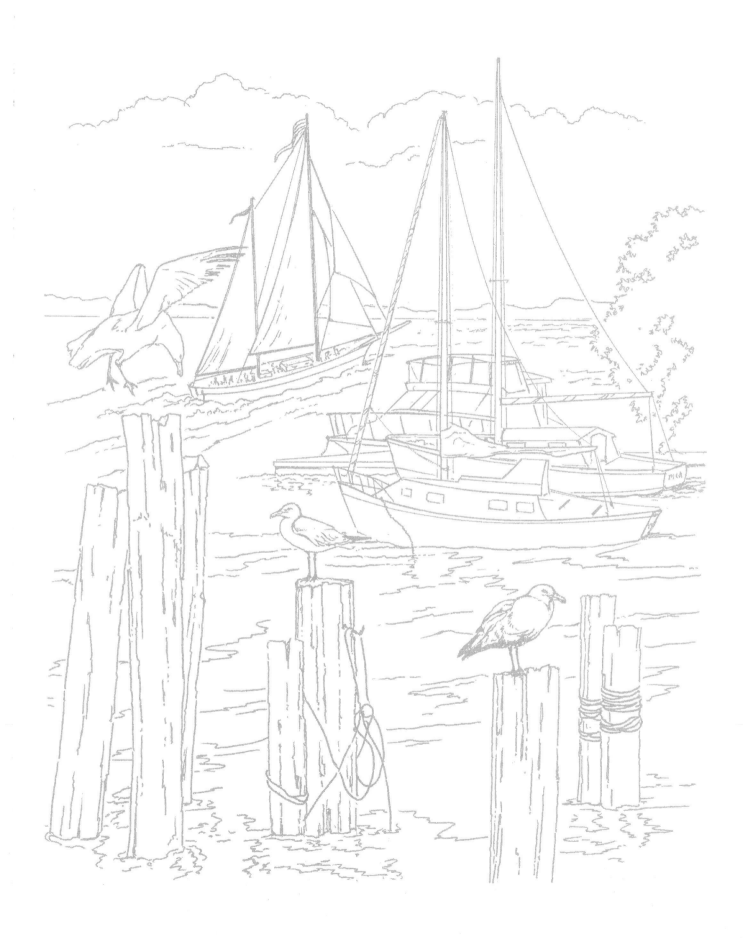

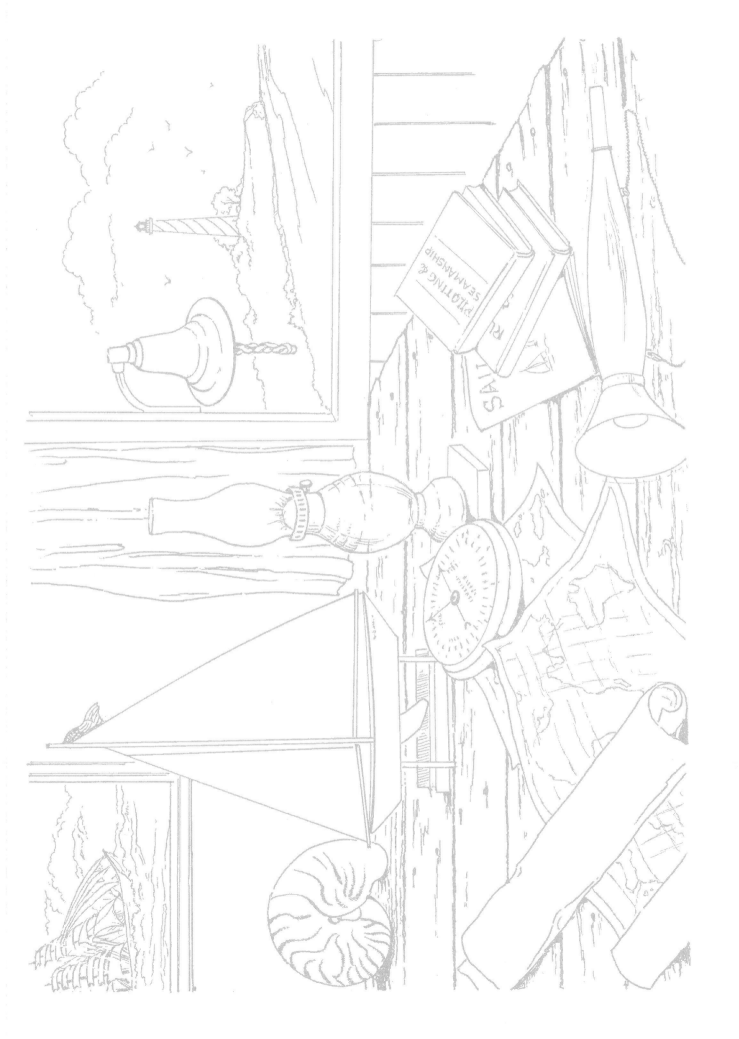

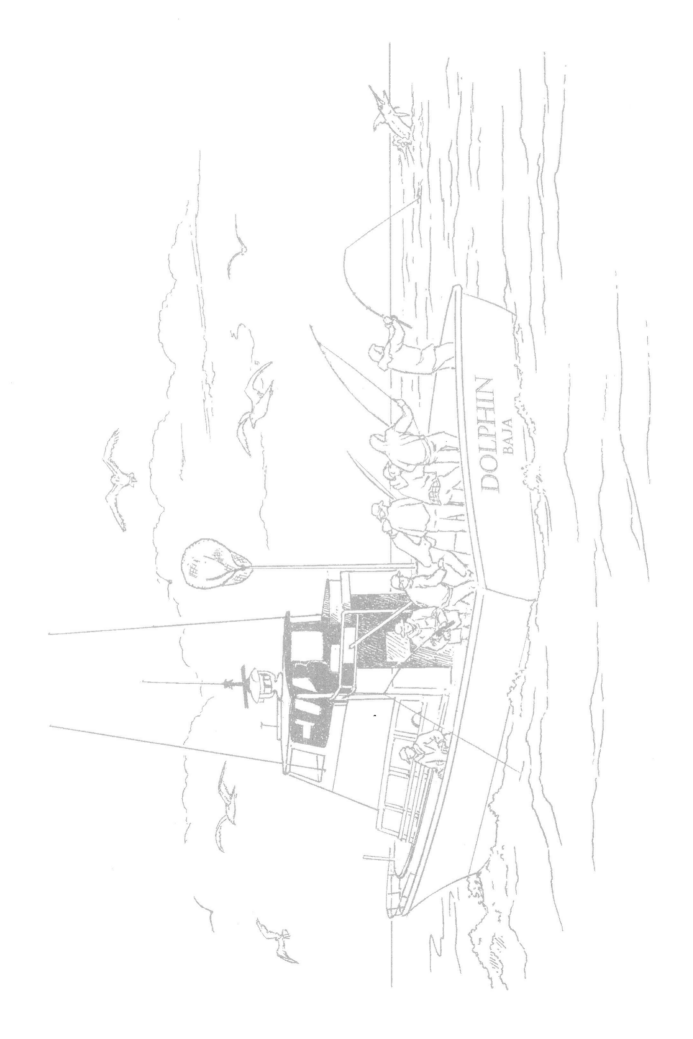

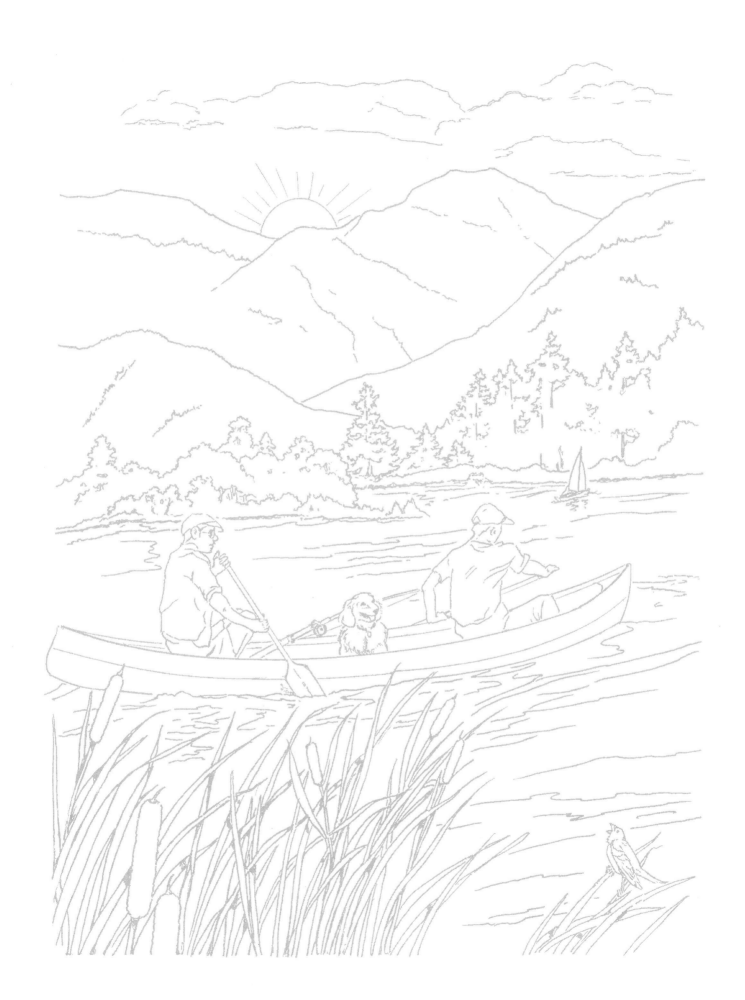

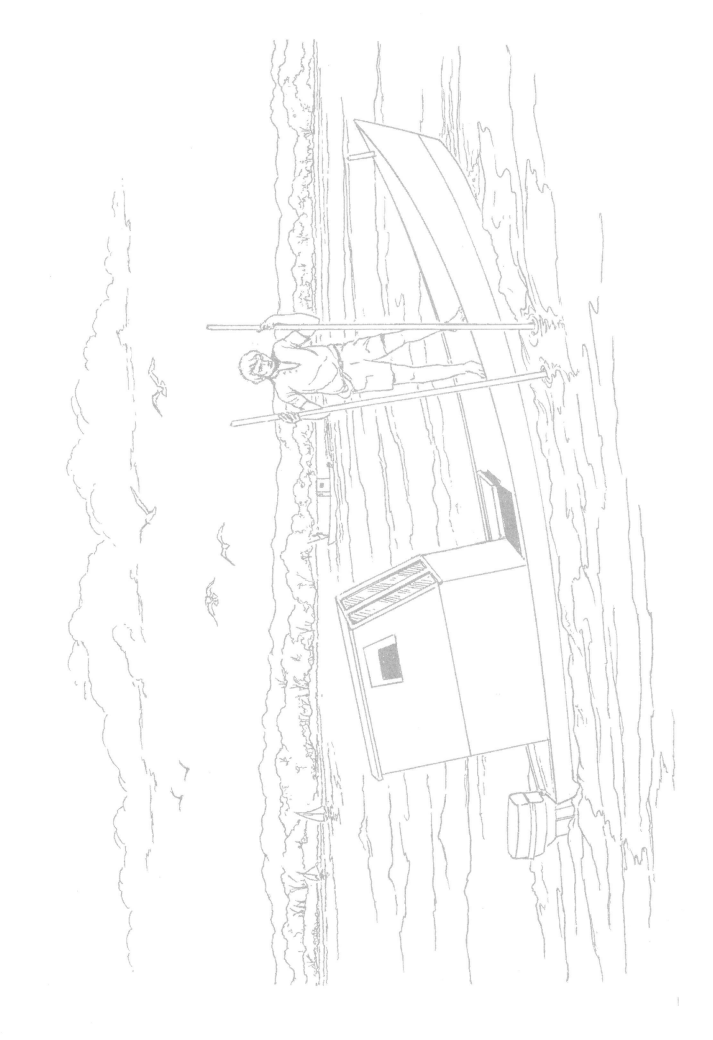

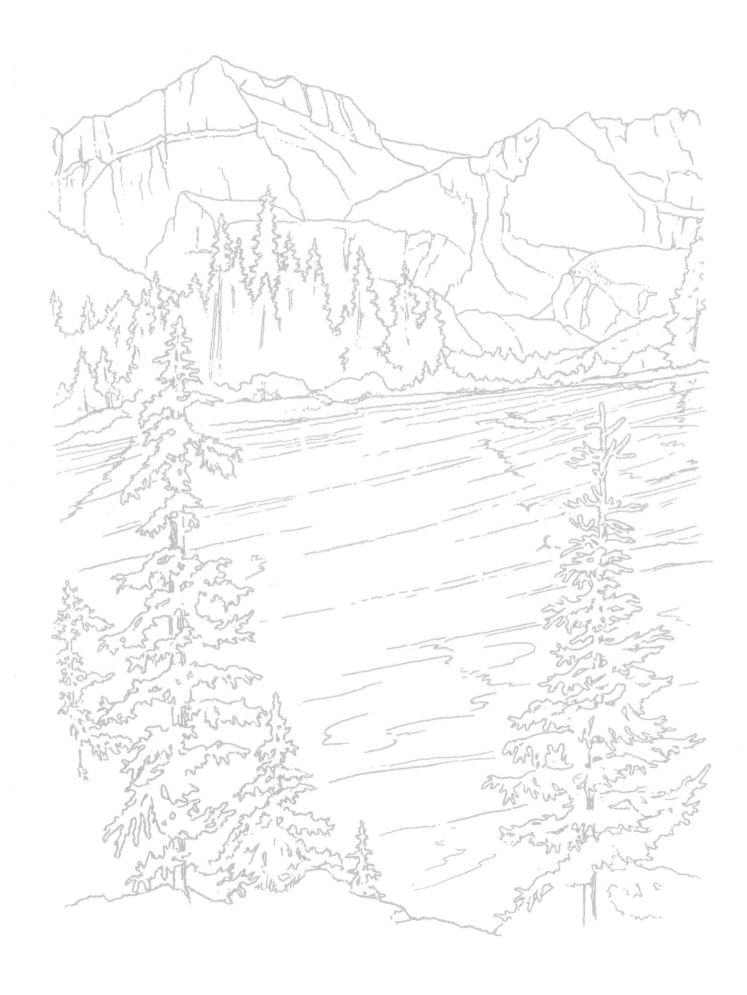

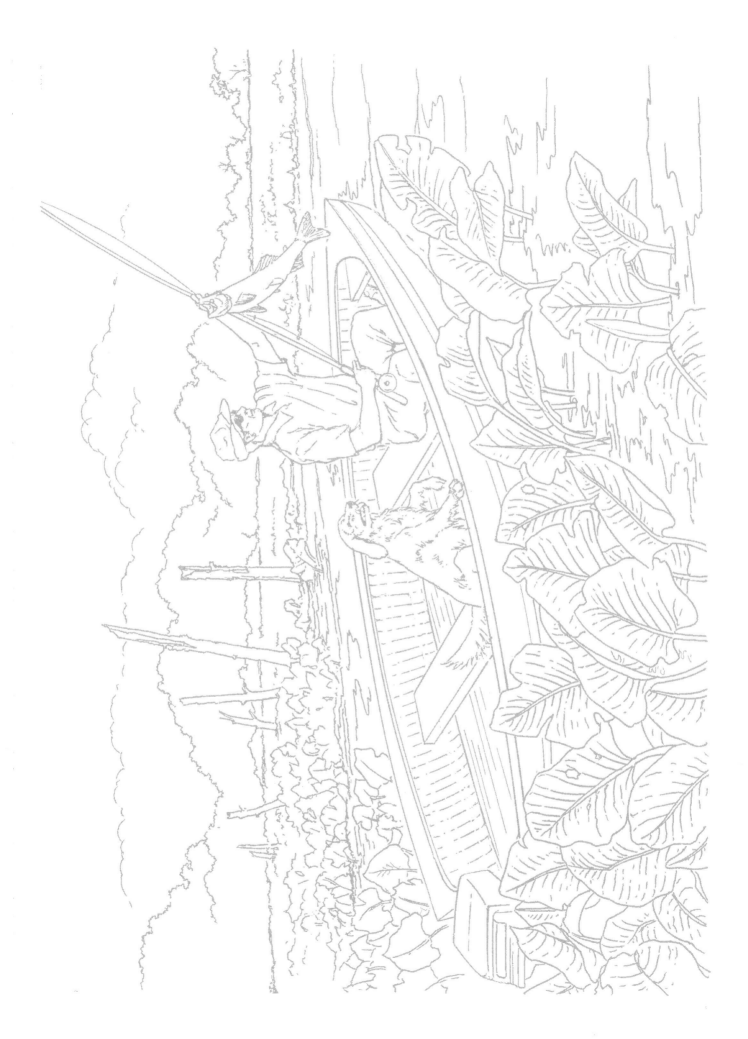

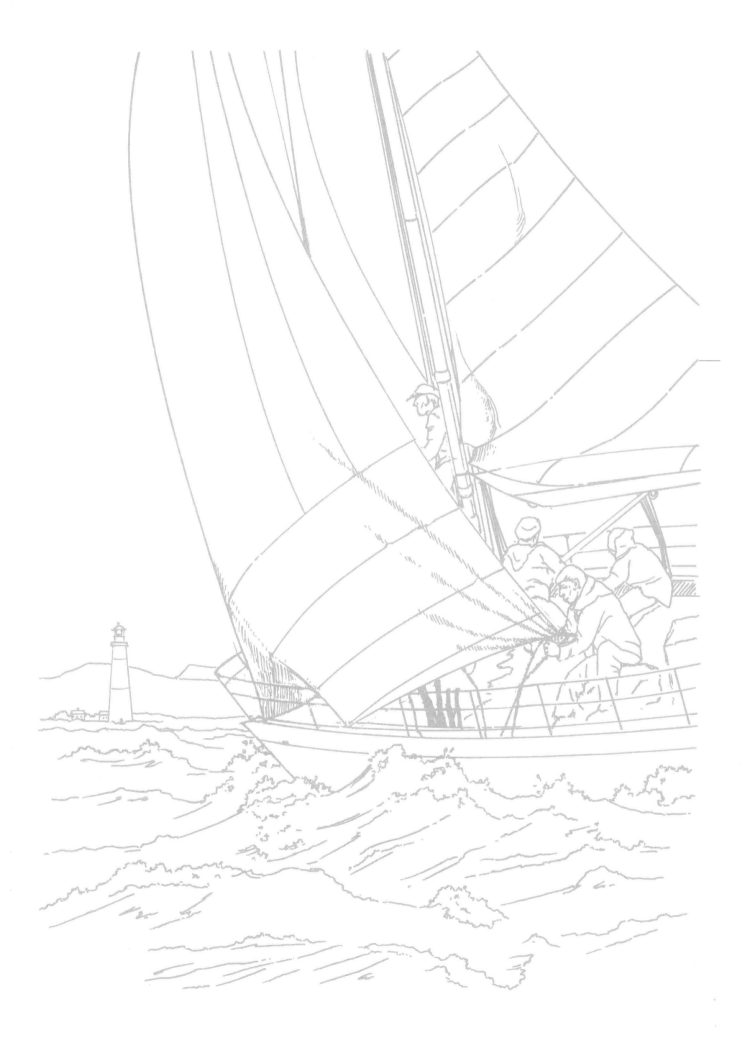

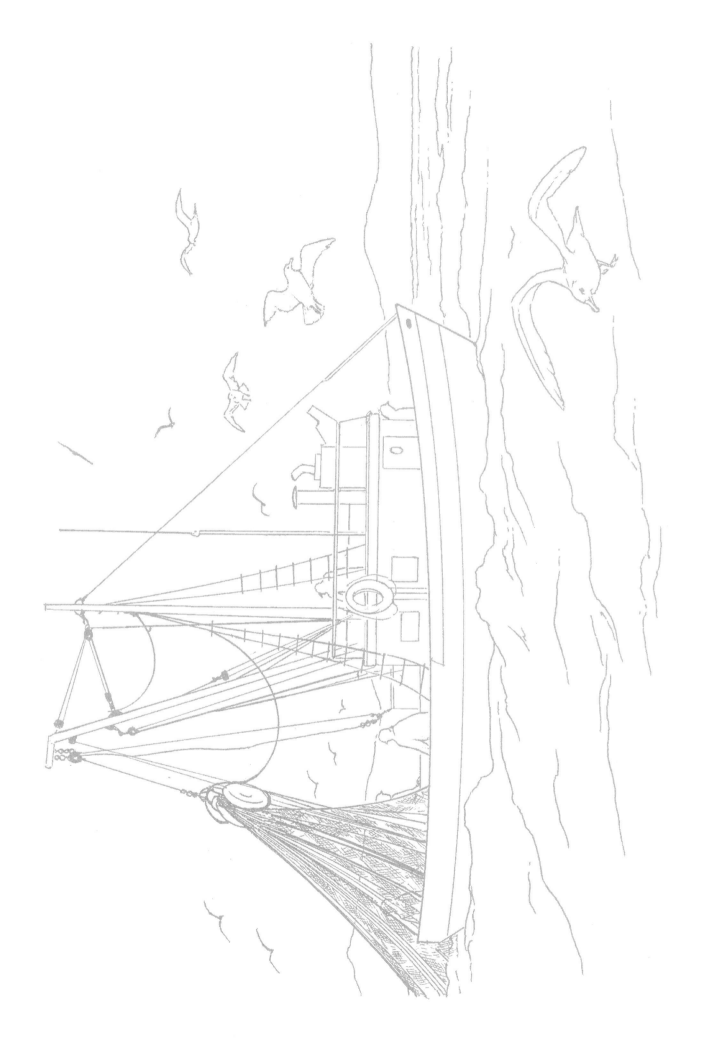

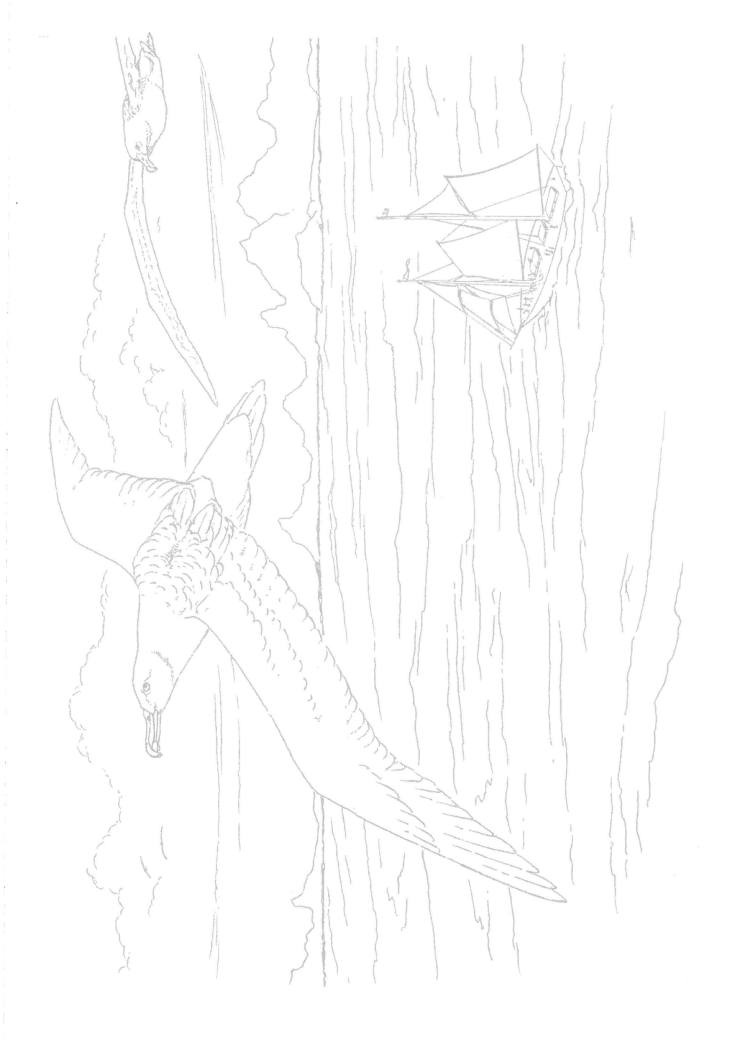

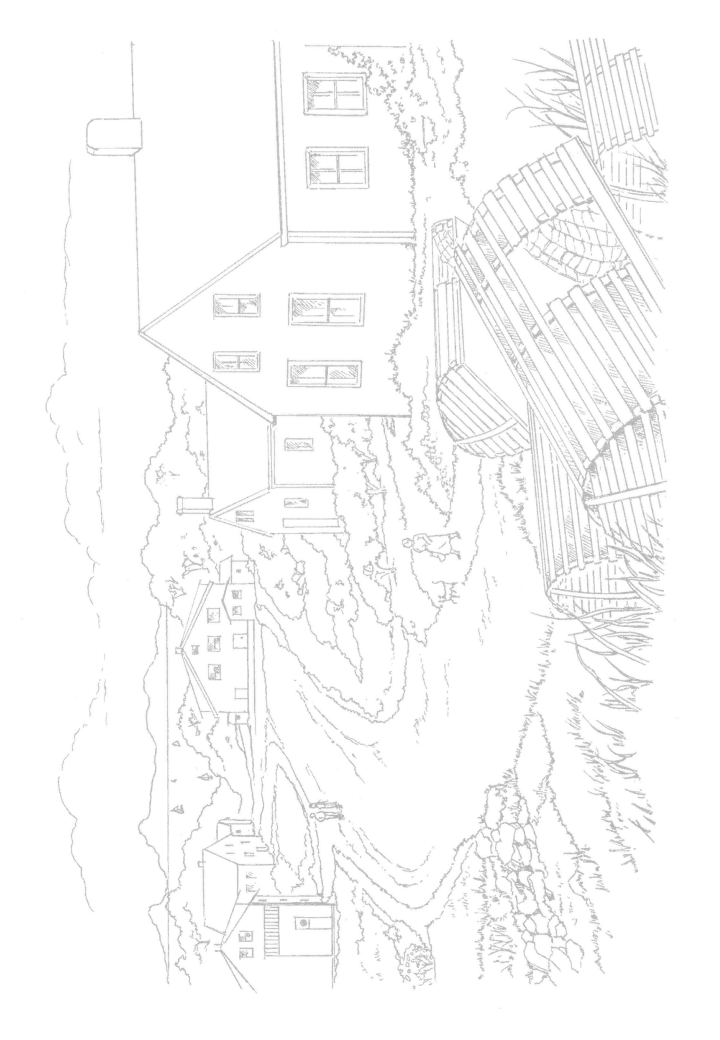

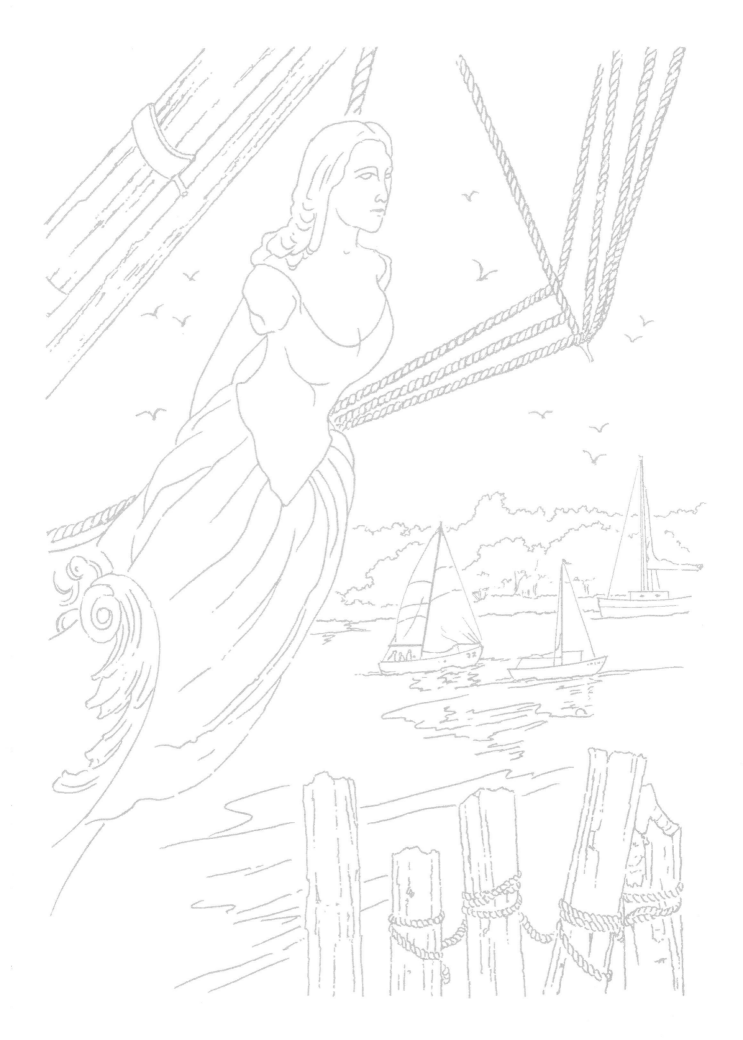

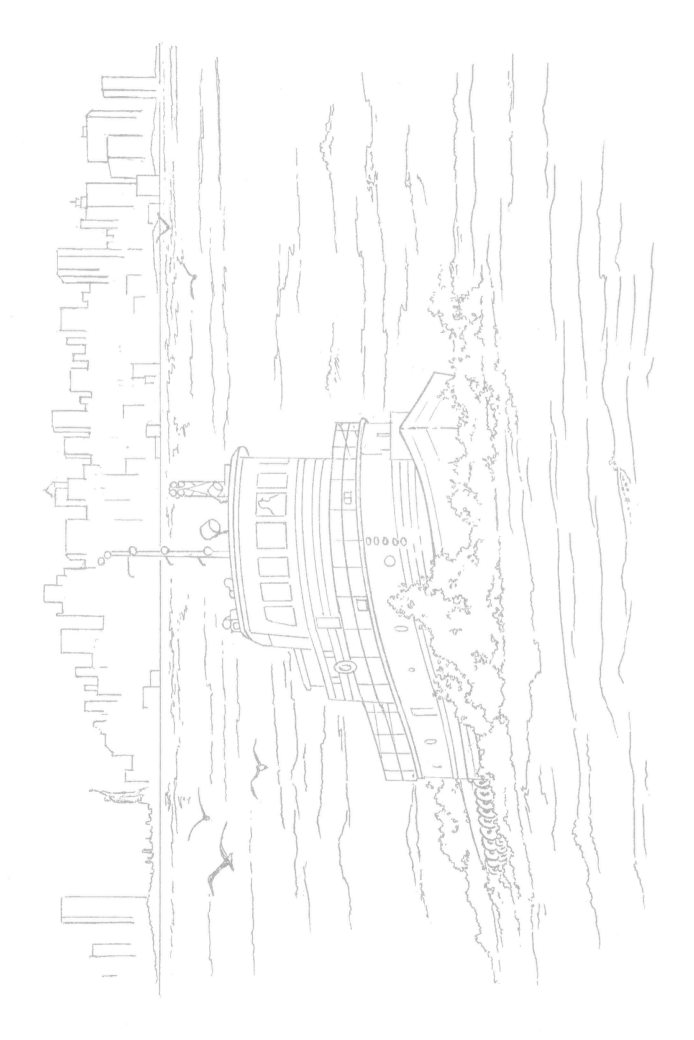

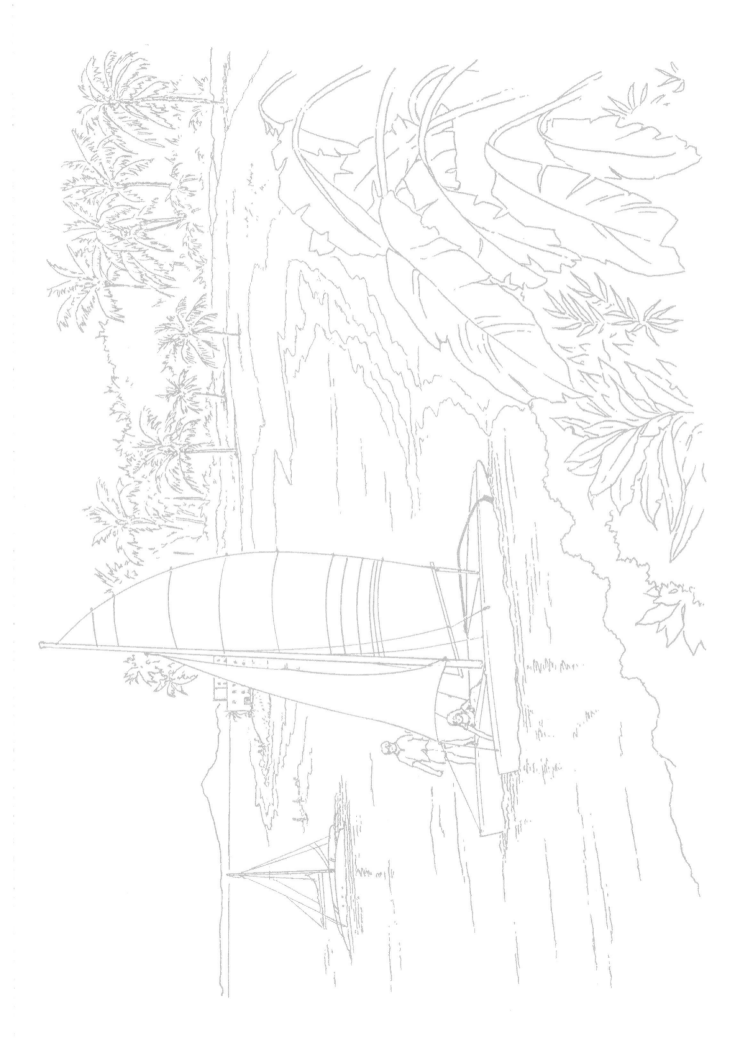

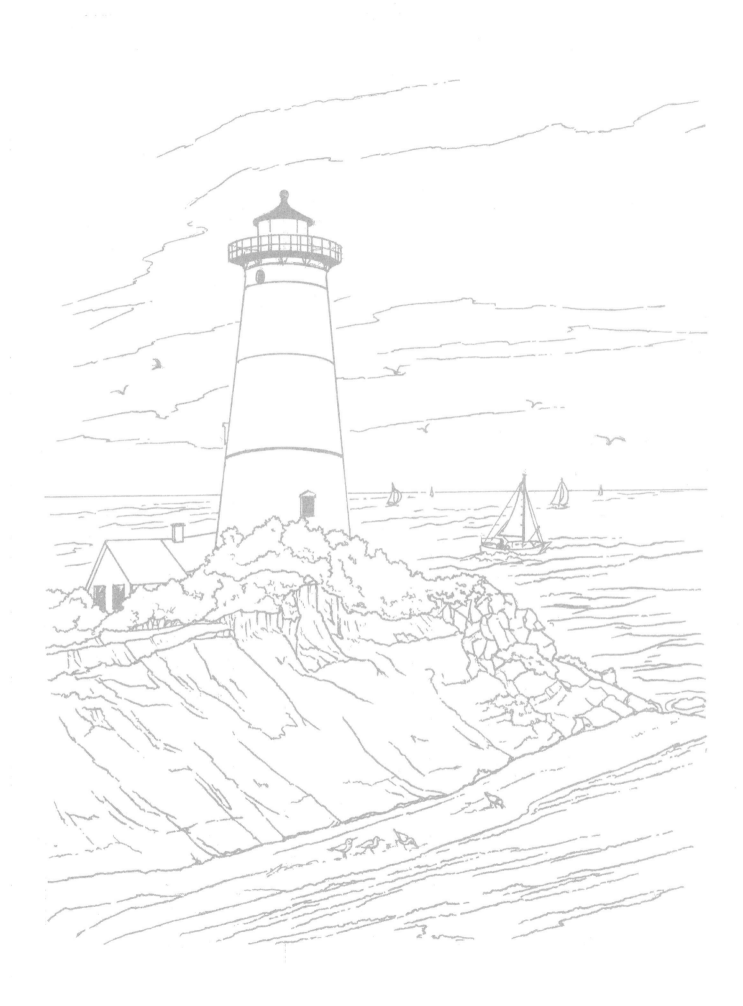

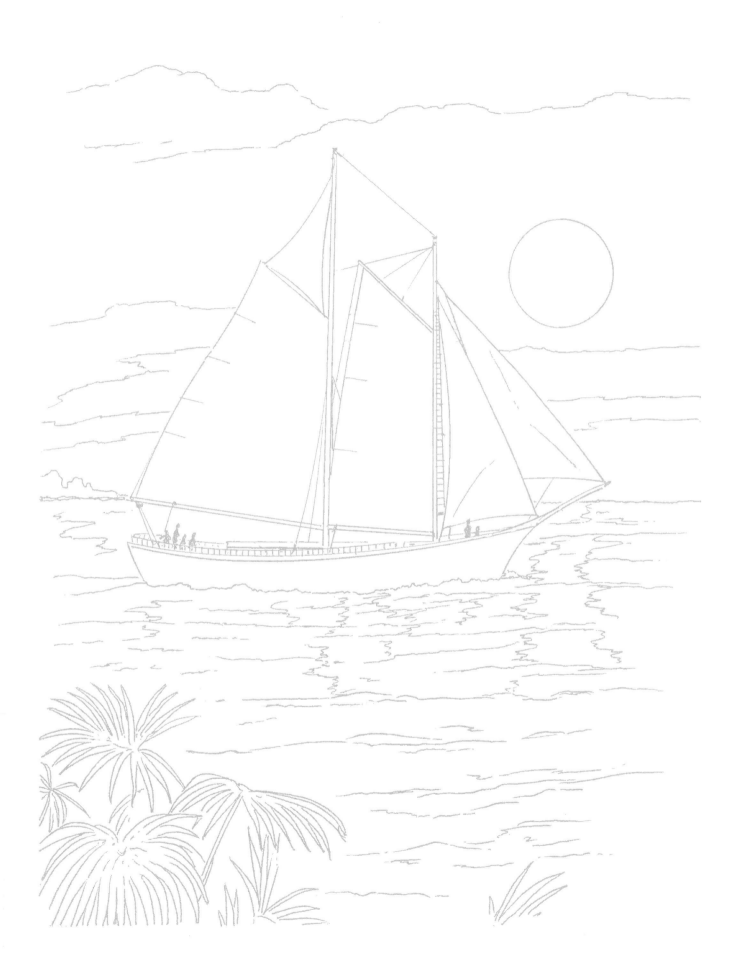

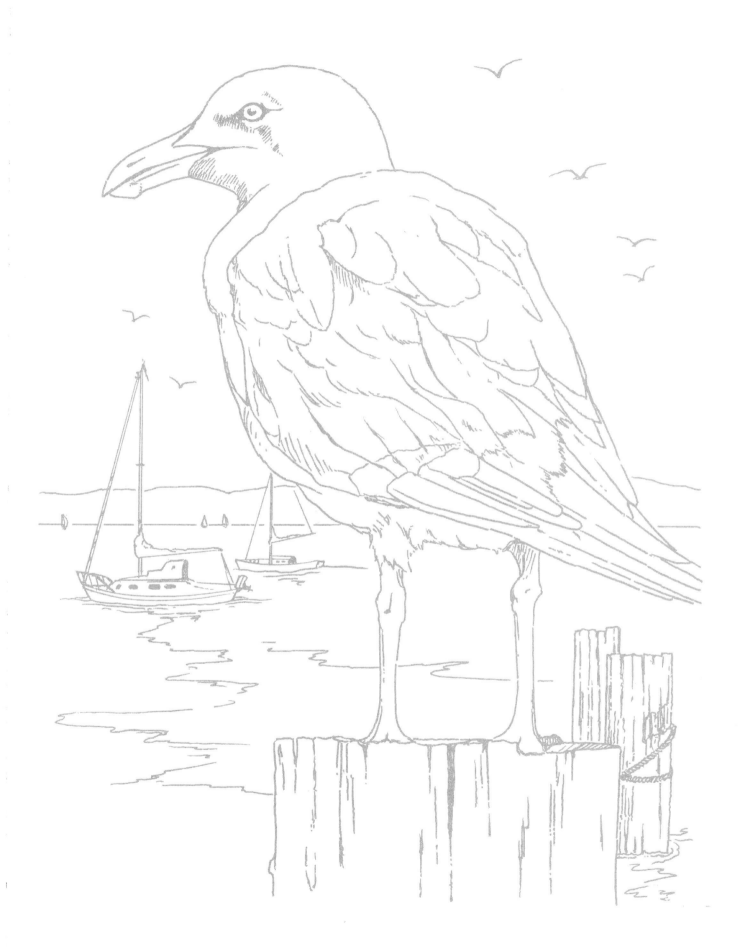